This book belongs to:

_____

_____

_____

READ ME
THE
HAGGADAH

written by
Chavie Freund

illustrated by
Tova Leff

CIS
P·U·B·L·I·S·H·E·R·S
New York · London · Jerusalem

A CIS PUBLICATION

Distributed in the U.S., Canada and overseas by
C.I.S. Publishers and Distributors
180 Park Avenue, Lakewood, New Jersey 08701
(201) 905-3000 Fax: (201) 367-6666

Distributed in Israel by
C.I.S. International (Israel)
Rechov Mishkalov 18/16
Har Nof, Jerusalem
Tel: 02-538-935

Distributed in the U.K. and Europe by
C.I.S. International (U.K.)
1 Palm Court, Queen Elizabeth Walk
London, England N16
Tel: 01-809-3723

Book and Cover Design by Ronda Kruger Israel

Printed in the United States of America

The ReadMe Series

The ReadMe Books are designed to introduce Jewish concepts to the pre-reader and the beginning reader in a clear and enjoyable children's presentation. The format and method of illustration have been developed through extensive consultation with leading *Rabbonim* and educators.

Read Me the Haggadah, the first in this series, is designed to enable the very young child to participate actively in the *Pesach Seder.* The highlights of the *Seder* are beautifully illustrated, and certain basic parts of the *Haggadah* have been included in the full Hebrew for the benefit of the beginning reader. The explanatory verses can be read to younger children, while beginners may be able to read the verses by themselves.

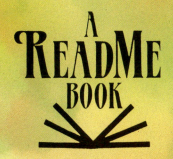

A **ReadMe** BOOK

Many years ago in Mitzrayim
There lived a king called Pharaoh
He made the Jews his slaves
And filled their lives with sorrow.

Each day they toiled and suffered
No rest did he allow them
And the labor and the beatings
Made them cry out to Hashem.

Hashem heard their cries
Of suffering and slavery
He sent the Mitzrim ten *makkos*
And set the Jewish people free.

That's why the *Yom Tov* of *Pesach*
Is a special celebration
Remember the miracles and thank Hashem
For the freedom to be His nation.

Bedikas Chametz/בְּדִיקַת חָמֵץ

When Hashem took us out of Mitzrayim
We left in such a haste
That the dough in our sacks
Had no time to become *chametz*.

We do *bedikas chametz*
The night before *Pesach* is here
To make sure after all the cleaning
That each nook is *chametz* clear.

Biur Chametz/בִּיעוּר חָמֵץ

On the morning of *Erev Pesach*
Biur chametz is done
All *chametz* is thrown in the fire
Where it is burnt to the very last crumb.

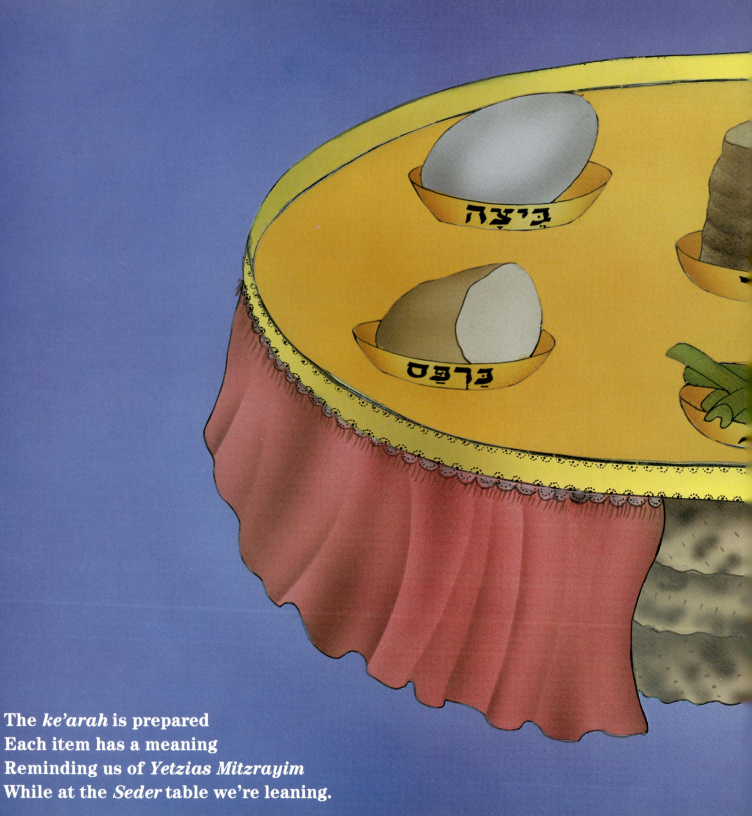

The *ke'arah* is prepared
Each item has a meaning
Reminding us of *Yetzias Mitzrayim*
While at the *Seder* table we're leaning.

Ke'arah/קְעָרָה

זְרוֹעַ

חֲרוֹסֶת

Zeroa, the bone, and *baitzah*, the egg
Help us remember when
In the *Bais Hamikdash* in Yerushalayim
We brought *korbanos* to Hashem.

Karpas, maror, charoses, chazeres
Are important to the *Seder*.
Each of these in the *ke'arah*
Will play its part later.

Seder night's a special order of things we say and do
To help us remember and feel as if we were set free, too!

קַדֵּשׁ

וּרְחַץ

כַּרְפַּס

יַחַץ

מַגִּיד

רָחְצָה

מוֹצִיא מַצָּה

מָרוֹר

כּוֹרֵךְ

שֻׁלְחָן עוֹרֵךְ

צָפוּן

בָּרֵךְ

הַלֵּל

נִרְצָה

Kadesh/קַדֵּשׁ

First comes *kaddeish*—we all make *kiddush*
"*Borei pri hagafen*," we recite
Over the first of four *kosos* of wine
That we will drink tonight.

בָּרוּךְ אַתָּה ה' אֱ־לֹהֵינוּ מֶלֶךְ הָעוֹלָם
בּוֹרֵא פְּרִי הַגָּפֶן:

Urchatz/וּרְחַץ

At *urchatz*, the father washes his hands
And since like a king he's treated
Water is brought to the table's head
To the place where he is seated.

בּוֹרֵא ... פְּרִי הָאֲדָמָה

Dip *karpas* in *mai melach*
Since salt water tastes like tears
Which the Jews shed in Mitzrayim
When they slaved so many years.

בָּרוּךְ אַתָּה ה' אֱ־לֹהֵינוּ מֶלֶךְ הָעוֹלָם
בּוֹרֵא פְּרִי הָאֲדָמָה:

At *yachatz*, we break the *matzoh*
Making sure it's the one in the middle
We save the larger part for *afikoman*
And put back the half that is little.

Quick! Hide the *afikoman*
Out of your father's sight
Then you can ask for a special prize
When he finds it later that night.

Magid/מַגִּיד

The main part of the *Seder* is *magid*
When we tell how Hashem's mighty hand
Took us from Mitzrayim
And gave us our very own land.

Ask and answer questions
Then all of us will see
How Hashem made many *nissim*
In order to set us free.

הָא לַחְמָא עַנְיָא

Pick up the *matzoh* and say
"This is the poor man's bread
Which we ate in Mitzrayim
Since more we were not fed."

We invite everyone to our *Seder*
The hungry and those in need
Next year may we be in Yerushalayim
And from this *galus* freed.

הָא לַחְמָא עַנְיָא.

דִּי אֲכָלוּ אַבְהָתָנָא בְּאַרְעָא דְמִצְרָיִם.

כָּל דִּכְפִין יֵיתֵי וְיֵיכוֹל.

כָּל דִּצְרִיךְ יֵיתֵי וְיִפְסַח.

הָשַׁתָּא הָכָא. לְשָׁנָה הַבָּאָה בְּאַרְעָא דְיִשְׂרָאֵל

הָשַׁתָּא עַבְדֵי. לְשָׁנָה הַבָּאָה בְּנֵי חוֹרִין:

Ma Nishtana/ מַה נִּשְׁתַּנָּה

So many new things we do and say
How different it all appears!
"Why *is* this night so different
From all nights of the year?"

All other nights we eat *chametz*
Or anything else that we choose
But tonight we eat only *matzoh*
And *chametz* we must refuse.

Many different vegetables
May be eaten throughout the year
But tonight we eat only *maror*
That's bitter and makes our eyes tear.

We know when we sit at the table
That dipping food is not too polite
But tonight we dip our food two times
Because it's the *Seder* night.

Whenever we come to the table
We may all sit up straight or lean
But tonight at the *Pesach Seder*
We recline like a king or queen.

מַה נִּשְׁתַּנָּה הַלַּיְלָה הַזֶּה מִכָּל הַלֵּילוֹת.

שֶׁבְּכָל הַלֵּילוֹת אָנוּ אוֹכְלִין חָמֵץ וּמַצָּה.
הַלַּיְלָה הַזֶּה כֻּלּוֹ מַצָּה.

שֶׁבְּכָל הַלֵּילוֹת אָנוּ אוֹכְלִין שְׁאָר יְרָקוֹת.
הַלַּיְלָה הַזֶּה כֻּלּוֹ מָרוֹר.

שֶׁבְּכָל הַלֵּילוֹת אֵין אָנוּ מַטְבִּילִין אֲפִילוּ פַּעַם אֶחָת.
הַלַּיְלָה הַזֶּה שְׁתֵּי פְעָמִים.

שֶׁבְּכָל הַלֵּילוֹת אָנוּ אוֹכְלִין בֵּין יוֹשְׁבִין וּבֵין מְסֻבִּין.
הַלַּיְלָה הַזֶּה כֻּלָּנוּ מְסֻבִּין.

Avadim Hayinu/עֲבָדִים הָיִינוּ

Now the Four Questions are answered
"*Avadim Hayinu*," we say
Hashem took us out of Mitzrayim
Many years ago on this day.

It's a *mitzvah* to talk all night
About how the Jewish people were saved
If Hashem had not taken us out
We'd all still be enslaved.

Baruch Hamakom/בָּרוּךְ הַמָּקוֹם

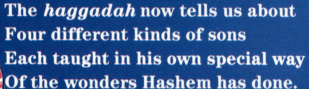

רָשָׁע

חָכָם

The *haggadah* now tells us about
Four different kinds of sons
Each taught in his own special way
Of the wonders Hashem has done.

Wise and good is the *chacham*
Torah fills his head
The *rasha* doesn't like *mitzvos*
He likes to poke fun instead.

The *tam* waits for an explanation
"What is all this?" he asks
The *she'aino yodaia lish'ol* asks nothing
To teach him is his parents' task.

שֶׁאֵינוֹ יוֹדֵעַ לִשְׁאוֹל

תָּם

לִכְבוֹד שַׁבָּת קֹדֶשׁ נֹאמַר

We thank Hashem for His promise
To Avraham Avinu long ago
That after four hundred years
Pharaoh would let us go.

Hashem said when the right time came
He would punish every Mitzri
And then with many treasures
The Jews would all go free.

Many times bad people have risen
And tried to destroy the Jews
But Hashem's promise has always saved us
And made our enemies lose.

וְהִיא שֶׁעָמְדָה לַאֲבוֹתֵינוּ וְלָנוּ.
שֶׁלֹּא אֶחָד בִּלְבַד עָמַד עָלֵינוּ לְכַלּוֹתֵנוּ.
אֶלָּא שֶׁבְּכָל דּוֹר וָדוֹר עוֹמְדִים עָלֵינוּ לְכַלּוֹתֵנוּ.
וְהַקָּדוֹשׁ בָּרוּךְ הוּא מַצִּילֵנוּ מִיָּדָם.

צֵא וּלְמַד

We now tell the story
Of one enemy Hashem saved us from
Lavan tried to destroy Yaakov
But he was overcome.

וַיֵּרֶד מִצְרַיְמָה

When Yaakov went down to Mitzrayim,
A small family he took along
But by the time Hashem took us out
We were many, great and strong.

Magid/מַגִּיד

בְּמְתֵי מְעָט

The Mitzrim wanted to make sure,
That the Jews would never escape
So they forced them to do such terrible work,
That it made their bodies ache!

The Mitzrim beat the Jews and whipped them
All newborn boys they tried to drown,
The Jews cried out to Hashem in pain
From the tortures all around.

Hashem knew the Jews must be freed
The right time for this had come

Eser Makos/עֶשֶׂר מַכּוֹת

He sent ten *makos* on Mitzrayim
For the evil things they had done.

Hashem did many more *nissim*
The *Yam Suf* He divided
He gave us *Shabbos* and the *Torah*
In the desert our needs He provided.

Dayeinu/דַּיֵּנוּ

For forty years in the *Midbar*
Mann from the sky He fed us
He built the *Bais Hamikdash*
And to Eretz Yisrael He led us.

"*Dayeinu*," we all sing,
As each wonder we recite,
It would have been enough for us
Each sign of special might.

Magid/מַגִּיד

פֶּסַח

מַצָּה

Pesach, matzoh and *Maror*
For the *korban, matzoh* and the bitter herbs.

Pesach means Hashem skipped over the Jews
When each first-born Mitzri He slew.

Our *matzoh* was baked in such haste
Because we left with no time to waste.

And the bitter *maror* is to symbolize
How the Mitzrim embittered our lives.

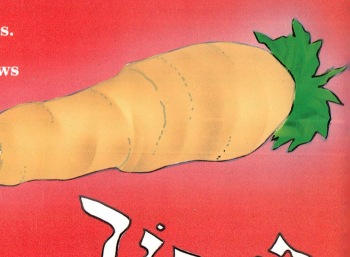

מָרוֹר

הַלֵּל עַבְדֵי ה׳ ...

Now we're almost finished with *magid*
To sing songs of praise it is time
We make a *berachah* and drink
The second *kos* of wine.

בָּרוּךְ אַתָּה ה׳ אֱ־לֹהֵינוּ מֶלֶךְ הָעוֹלָם
בּוֹרֵא פְּרִי הַגָּפֶן:

Rachtzah/רָחְצָה
Motzi Matzoh/מוֹצִיא מַצָּה

עַל נְטִילַת יָדִים ...

The time has come for *rachtzah*
We wash each hand and dry it
Make a *berachah* and wait for the *matzoh*
And make sure we keep very quiet!

בָּרוּךְ אַתָּה ה׳ אֱ-לֹהֵינוּ מֶלֶךְ הָעוֹלָם
אֲשֶׁר קִדְּשָׁנוּ בְּמִצְוֹתָיו וְצִוָּנוּ
עַל נְטִילַת יָדָיִם:

בָּרוּךְ אַתָּה ה׳ אֱ-לֹהֵינוּ מֶלֶךְ הָעוֹלָם
הַמּוֹצִיא לֶחֶם מִן הָאָרֶץ:

בָּרוּךְ אַתָּה ה׳ אֱ-לֹהֵינוּ מֶלֶךְ הָעוֹלָם
אֲשֶׁר קִדְּשָׁנוּ בְּמִצְוֹתָיו וְצִוָּנוּ
עַל אֲכִילַת מַצָּה:

הַמּוֹצִיא לֶחֶם מִן הָאָרֶץ

מַצָּה

We wash and make three *berachos*
For the *matzoh* we will eat
Make sure while you eat your *kezayis*
To lean to the left of your seat.

Maror/מָרוֹר

Now the *maror* and *chazeres* are eaten
Al Achillas Maror is said
We dip it in *charoses*
Whose color is brick-red.

Yes, *maror* and *charoses* together
Remind us of the bitter time
The Mitzrim forced us to make red bricks
Out of mortar and of lime.

"This is what Hillel did," we say
"In the *Bais Hamikdash* time"
When he made a special sandwich
Of *matzoh* and *maror* combined.

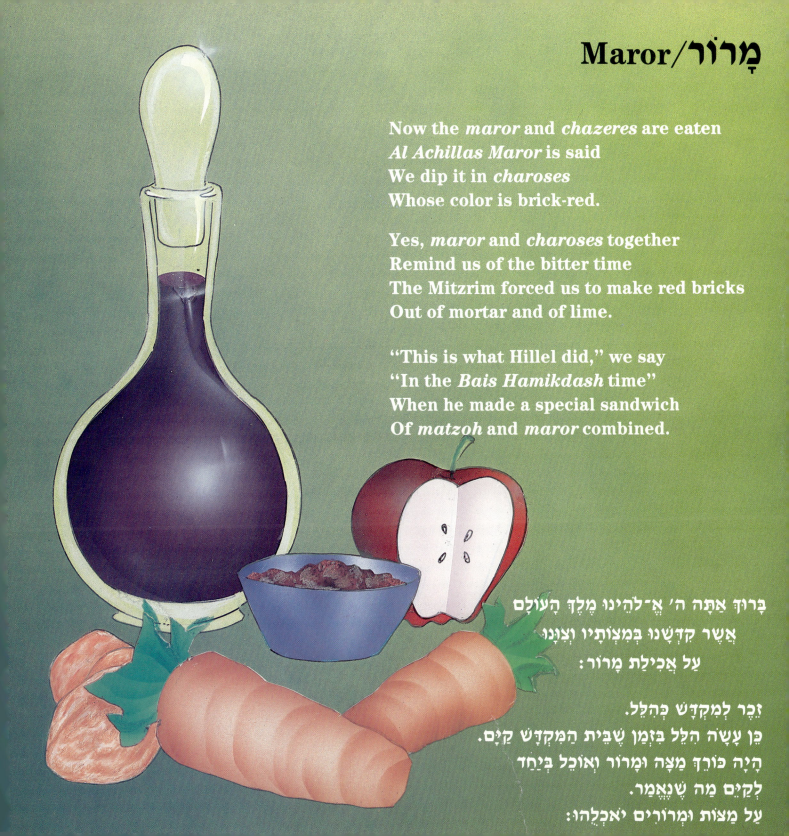

בָּרוּךְ אַתָּה ה' אֱ-לֹהֵינוּ מֶלֶךְ הָעוֹלָם
אֲשֶׁר קִדְּשָׁנוּ בְּמִצְוֹתָיו וְצִוָּנוּ
עַל אֲכִילַת מָרוֹר:

זֵכֶר לְמִקְדָּשׁ כְּהִלֵּל.
כֵּן עָשָׂה הִלֵּל בִּזְמַן שֶׁבֵּית הַמִּקְדָּשׁ קַיָּם.
הָיָה כּוֹרֵךְ מַצָּה וּמָרוֹר וְאוֹכֵל בְּיַחַד
לְקַיֵּם מַה שֶׁנֶּאֱמַר.
עַל מַצּוֹת וּמְרוֹרִים יֹאכְלֻהוּ:

Shulchan Orech/שֻׁלְחָן עוֹרֵך

The *Yom Tov* meal is eaten
But make sure you leave room
To eat the *afikoman*
That will be brought out soon!

We have no *Korban Pesach*
The *afikoman* takes its place
After that nothing may be eaten
So we won't forget its taste.

Birchas Hamazon/בִּרְכַּת הַמָּזוֹן

Then comes *Birchas Hamazon*
We say each word carefully
And afterwards, we make a *berachah*
And drink *kos* number three.

בָּרוּךְ אַתָּה ה' אֱ־לֹהֵינוּ מֶלֶךְ הָעוֹלָם הַזָּן
אֶת הָעוֹלָם כֻּלּוֹ בְּטוּבוֹ בְּחֵן בְּחֶסֶד וּבְרַחֲמִים
הוּא נוֹתֵן לֶחֶם לְכָל בָּשָׂר כִּי לְעוֹלָם חַסְדּוֹ.
וּבְטוּבוֹ הַגָּדוֹל תָּמִיד לֹא חָסַר לָנוּ וְאַל יֶחְסַר
לָנוּ מָזוֹן לְעוֹלָם וָעֶד. בַּעֲבוּר שְׁמוֹ הַגָּדוֹל כִּי
הוּא אֵ־ל זָן וּמְפַרְנֵס לַכֹּל וּמֵטִיב לַכֹּל וּמֵכִין
מָזוֹן לְכָל בְּרִיּוֹתָיו אֲשֶׁר בָּרָא. (כָּאָמוּר פּוֹתֵחַ
אֶת יָדֶךָ וּמַשְׂבִּיעַ לְכָל חַי רָצוֹן). בָּרוּךְ אַתָּה
ה' הַזָּן אֶת הַכֹּל:
נוֹדֶה לְךָ . . .

שְׁפֹךְ חֲמָתְךָ/Shefoch Chamascha

שְׁפֹךְ חֲמָתֶךָ

שְׁפֹךְ

Shefoch Chamascha is said
While keeping open the door
We do this in order to show
That of Hashem's protection we're sure.

שְׁפֹךְ חֲמָתְךָ אֶל הַגּוֹיִם אֲשֶׁר לֹא יְדָעוּךָ וְעַל מַמְלָכוֹת
אֲשֶׁר בְּשִׁמְךָ לֹא קָרָאוּ. כִּי אָכַל אֶת יַעֲקֹב וְאֶת נָוֵהוּ
הֵשַׁמּוּ. שְׁפָךְ עֲלֵיהֶם זַעְמֶךָ וַחֲרוֹן אַפְּךָ יַשִּׂיגֵם. תִּרְדֹּף
בְּאַף וְתַשְׁמִידֵם מִתַּחַת שְׁמֵי ה':

Hallel/הַלֵּל

הַלְלוּ אֶת ה' כָּל גּוֹיִם

We sing *Hallel* to thank Hashem
And praise Him for His creation,
May the day soon come when His name is praise[d]
By every single nation!

We make a *berachah* and drink
The fourth and last *kos* of wine
We say *Al Hagefen* to thank Hashem
For creating the fruits of the vine.

בָּרוּךְ אַתָּה ה׳ אֱ-לֹהֵינוּ מֶלֶךְ הָעוֹלָם
בּוֹרֵא פְּרִי הַגָּפֶן:

בִּירוּשָׁלָֽיִם

Chasal Siddur Pesach
The *Seder's* end now draws near
We ask Hashem to send us *Mashiach*
In a rebuilt Yerushalayim next year.

חֲסַל סִדּוּר פֶּסַח כְּהִלְכָתוֹ. כְּכָל מִשְׁפָּטוֹ וְחֻקָּתוֹ.
כַּאֲשֶׁר זָכִינוּ לְסַדֵּר אוֹתוֹ כֵּן נִזְכֶּה לַעֲשׂוֹתוֹ.
זָךְ שׁוֹכֵן מְעוֹנָה. קוֹמֵם קְהַל עֲדַת מִי מָנָה.
בְּקָרוֹב נַהֵל נִטְעֵי כַנָּה. פְּדוּיִם לְצִיּוֹן בְּרִנָּה.